When I first read Deepak Chopra's *Seven Spiritual Laws for Parents*, I was deeply inspired to share these important messages with my own children and students. While I found many lovely stories in bookstores and libraries, I never quite found children's stories infused with the essence of the *Seven Spiritual Laws*, so I wrote them myself! I'm excited now to be able to share these stories with children of all ages all over the world. I hope you enjoy them as much as we have! Blessings, Lora Ann.

Deepak Chopra's
Seven Spiritual Laws for Parents

First Spiritual Law:
"Everything is possible."

Second Spiritual Law:
"If you want to get something, give it."

Third Spiritual Law:
"When you make a choice, you change the future."

Fourth Spiritual Law:
"Don't say no — go with the flow."

Fifth Spiritual Law:
"Every time you wish or want, you plant a seed."

Sixth Spiritual Law:
"Enjoy the journey."

Seventh Spiritual Law:
"You arc here for a reason."

For Savana and Zack
You are my angels.
Thank you for bringing heaven to earth.

Text copyright ©2005 by Lora Ann
Illustrations copyright ©2005 by Hannah Rose Shaffer

Library of Congress Control Number: 2005922227
ISBN 0-9764724-0-6
Printed in China
First LikeMinds™ Edition, April 2005

www.likemindspress.com

Seven Stories to Live By

by Lora Ann

Inspired by Deepak Chopra's
Seven Spiritual Laws for Parents

Illustrations by Hannah Shaffer

Table of Contents

Two Points and Counting! (First Spiritual Law)............2

The Gift of Friendship (Second Spiritual Law) 12

Suki's Choice (Third Spiritual Law)............................. 20

A Game for Hannah (Fourth Spiritual Law) 26

Tara Plants a Seed (Fifth Spiritual Law) 34

The Lucky Tee (Sixth Spiritual Law) 40

The Scavenger Hunt (Seventh Spiritual Law)............. 48

Glossary 58

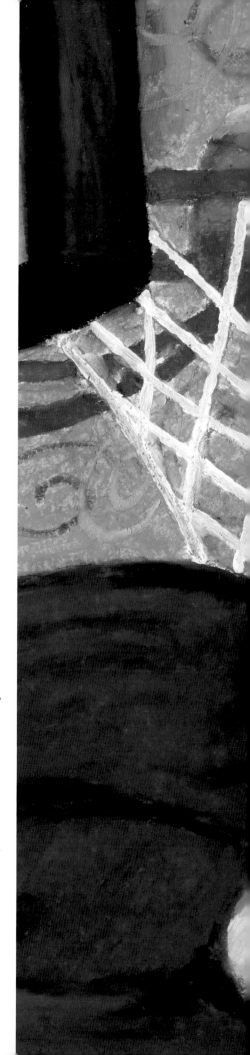

Two Points and Counting!

First Spiritual Law:
"Everything is possible."

Diego loved to play basketball. Well, he loved the idea of playing basketball, anyway. Every day it was the same routine — home from school, snack with Mama, and out to the backyard to practice.

Diego loved his after-school snacks with Mama. He thought of this as his special time with her. She would serve something healthy and yummy like celery and peanut butter, carrots, or apple slices. Celery and peanut butter was Diego's favorite, especially when Mama sprinkled raisins on top.

While they sat down to eat, Mama would check in with him about how school was going.

"After all," she would smile and say, "it's not easy being a second grader."

Diego would give Mama the latest scoop on how it was going with his friends, what he learned that day at school, and especially his

2

math. Math was not his favorite subject, but Mama always reminded him that he could be good at anything he tried.

"Everything is possible, *hijo*," she would say with a hug.

"Mama," sighed Diego, "if you didn't remind me of that practically every day, I just might forget."

"Well, good thing you have me here just for that!" Mama winked.

After, Diego would tuck the heavy orange ball under his right arm and grab a cookie on his way out the door. He liked to call it his after-snack snack.

"One for the road!" he'd say over his shoulder as he headed out the back door.

In the backyard he'd hold the leather ball up to his chest, squint up toward the basket, and aim. He'd bend his knees a little, close his eyes, and give a little jump as he threw the ball up to the basket.

Then he'd watch as the ball went around, to the side, to the backboard, under, over, just about everywhere except through the net.

But Diego was determined. Some days he stayed in the backyard practicing until dinner time. When the ball came back down without going through the hoop, Diego would take a deep breath, dribble the ball, and try again. He was getting closer, he could feel it.

He had been coming to his backyard every afternoon for a few weeks, ever since he had gotten the new ball for his seventh birthday. His older brother, Carlos, liked to tease him, saying he had never made an official basket yet.

Diego didn't let that bother him — not much anyway. He could see the ball dropping smoothly through the hoop in his imagination. Sometimes he'd lie in bed at night imagining a cheering crowd and hearing the announcer shout, "It was nothin' but net for Diego Diaz! He has done it again!"

"Nothin' but net" was Diego's dream. Carlos always told him that if he could imagine it, he could do it. Diego could just see the ball slipping over the hoop and through the net. Carlos reminded him to keep seeing it in his mind and he would make it happen on the court.

Then he would echo the words that Mama told them so often, "Everything is possible."

Diego was beginning to wonder if that was really true for him, at least when it came to basketball, but he just kept imagining the ball hitting the hoop and falling through the net.

One breezy, fall afternoon when Diego was in the backyard, he heard a chopping noise nearby.

Clip, clip, clip.

He looked over the tall bushes and into the yard next door. At first he didn't see anything.

Snip, snip, snip.

He put down his basketball and stood on a chair to look over the fence to see where the noise was coming from. That's when he saw him.

On the other side of the fence was a man with white hair and a beard, bent over, clip-clip-clipping away at his own rose bushes with the same kind of big scissors Diego had seen his mother using in her garden.

"So that's the new neighbor," Diego said to himself.

"Hi there!" Diego smiled and waved to the man.

Diego had gained a reputation as the friendliest kid on the block. He was always making new friends and was known for being fun, fair, and easy to get along with.

"I'm Diego," he added. "You must be the new neighbor!"

The man just kept snipping away without looking up. Diego shrugged and sat down to eat his extra cookie.

Most days after that Diego noticed the neighbor working in his backyard. One day he'd be mowing the grass, other days pulling weeds, snipping the bushes, or turning the soil.

Diego always waved and yelled, "Hi" or "How are ya?" But the neighbor never answered. He always seemed to be concentrating on his gardening.

Diego would practice his shots until he was tired and then sit down for his after-snack snack, the cookie.

One night, after two solid weeks of practicing, Diego sat at dinner resting his face on his fist, his fork barely touching his food.

"*Hijo*, if you push that rice and chicken around your plate anymore, it's going to fall right off," said Mama. "I didn't make your favorite *arroz con pollo* just to watch the rice and chicken fall off your plate."

Diego sighed. "I just feel like I'm never going to get the ball in the hoop. Maybe I just can't do it." Diego threw his hands in the air with frustration and added, "It just seems impossible!"

Mama leaned over and put her arm around Diego's

shoulders.

"Diego, everything's possible. You were doing great last time you and Carlos practiced together. You're getting really close," she said. "You just have to keep practicing. Remember when your sister was learning how to do a cartwheel?"

Diego chuckled at the thought of his sister, Gabi, practicing her cartwheels last year. She landed on everything but her feet.

Just then Gabi cleared her throat dramatically, "A-hem. If you've noticed, now I can do a perfect cartwheel anytime, anywhere, with a great landing."

She stood up and put her hands in the air. "Should I demonstrate?"

"That's okay, Gabi," said Mama. "No gymnastics during dinner, please."

Mama smiled and gave Diego a hug. "*Hijito*, you have the right idea. You can do it, just keep practicing."

"That's right," Carlos chimed in. "Even the pros have to practice. Maybe you'll be a pro someday. Like Mama says, everything's —"

"I know, I know," interrupted Diego. "Everything's possible."

The next afternoon Diego was at it again. He dribbled, he aimed, he kept his eyes on the basket, and he tossed the ball up. The ball went up, up, up to the hoop, rolled on the rim, and rolled right off the side and back down.

"Aaahhh!" Diego sighed. "So close!"

He grabbed the ball and flopped down on a backyard chair. He was pooped. His arms ached. He was tired of practicing and he was tired of missing the hoop!

"Someday it's going to be nothin' but net," he said as he sat up tall in the chair and looked over the fence. It looked like the old man was planting something.

"Whatcha planting?" he yelled. No answer. "Mister?" Diego shrugged and went back to his practice.

"Someday, he might even answer me," Diego muttered to himself.

The next day Diego felt different. He felt confident as he made an announcement. "Today's the day," he said as he dipped his cookie into a cold glass of milk.

"The day for what, *hijito*?" asked Mama as he started out the back door with his cookie and ball.

On his way out, he stopped to grab an extra cookie and said, "I have an idea."

In the backyard he started his practice just like always. But today, he felt different. He felt prepared and confident. He looked at the rim, aimed, and shot the ball up.

The ball went up just like always. This time it didn't hit the backboard. This time it didn't roll around the rim.

This time it glided right over the rim and through the hoop. It swished back and forth against the net as it fell through, bounced once, and landed in Diego's surprised hands.

He was so surprised he just stood holding the ball, his brown eyes wide with amazement. Then he realized what just happened. He had finally made a basket!

"Woo-hoo!" he yelled as he jumped up and down.

"That was a great shot!" he heard a voice say from next door. But this voice couldn't belong to the neighbor. It was a girl's voice.

Still excited, Diego looked over the bushes to see a young girl about his age standing next to the old man next door.

"Did you see that?" Diego asked excitedly as he walked closer to the girl.

"Do you live here too?" he asked. "Oh yeah," he added as he wiped his hand and held it out to shake her hand, "I'm Diego."

"I'm Miranda," said the girl, shaking Diego's hand. "I don't live here, I'm just visiting my grandpa," she said as she pointed to the neighbor. "He moved here to be closer to all of us grandchildren," she added.

Then she turned to her grandfather and made some hand motions as she said, "*Abuelo*, this is Diego, he likes to play basketball."

The man used his hands to say something back to Miranda and they both laughed.

"Is that sign language?" asked Diego. "We learned the sign-language alphabet in school last year."

"Grandpa can't hear," answered Miranda. "Everyone in my family knows how to sign so we can talk to him. He says he's noticed that you don't like to play basketball, you LOVE to play basketball! He's seen you practicing lots of times." Miranda was using her hands to make sure her grandfather knew what she was telling Diego.

The neighbor signed a message back to Miranda and she said, "That would be great, *Abuelo*!"

She turned to Diego and continued to use her hands as she said, "He says he used to be quite a basketball player in his day and that next time you practice, he'll teach you a hook shot, if you want."

She continued to watch Grandpa's hands and told Diego what he was saying.

"His name is Samuel, but he says you can call him Señor Sam. That's what all his friends call him."

Diego shot his winning smile to Señor Sam. "I'd love to learn a hook shot," he said as Miranda signed the words. "And I can't wait to learn more sign language so that I can talk to Señor Sam myself."

Just then Diego remembered the cookie. "Hold on!" he said as he ran to the table and back.

"I almost forgot, this is for you," he said as he held the cookie out to Señor Sam.

Diego used his fingers to spell out c-o-o-k-i-e. Señor Sam smiled and signed a word that Diego knew meant "thank you."

"Do you really think you'll learn more sign language?" asked Miranda.

"Of course!" Diego answered as he looked over his shoulder at the basketball hoop with a smile. "You know what they say, everything is possible!"

The Gift of Friendship

Second Spiritual Law:

"If you want to get something, give it."

One day at school, Dakota's teacher, Ms. Luna, made an announcement. She stood at the front of the class behind a boy that Dakota had never seen before.

Ms. Luna rested her hands lightly on the boy's shoulders as she announced, "Class, this is Ben. I hope you'll all help him feel welcome," she said as she showed Ben his desk and books.

"Dakota," she added, "will you show Ben around our school this week? Make sure he knows where to go, where to put his things, where to get the supplies he needs."

"Sure," Dakota answered. Ms. Luna had asked him to do things like this before. She always reminded him that he was a great leader and a good friend. Dakota always felt important when Ms. Luna gave him jobs like this.

At recess Dakota and his friend Antonio asked Ben if he wanted to play marbles with them. Ben watched them play for a minute before he answered. "Nah, you guys are probably no good anyway. I don't want to waste my time playing with a bunch of losers," he said.

Antonio's face turned red the way it always did when he was

angry. "Oh yeah?" he said as he squinted his eyes at Ben. "Well, we don't really want to play with the stinky new kid anyway."

Ben didn't answer. He just kicked the dirt and walked away.

Antonio gathered up all the marbles and turned to Dakota. "C'mon," he said, "let's get out of here."

"Yeah, but I'm supposed to be showing him around today. It's my job!" Dakota followed Ben to the spot where some kids were playing four-square.

When Sophie, Joey, and Aiyana saw Ben watching their game, they asked him if he wanted to play. Ben said that four-square was a baby game and he wasn't going to play any dumb old baby game.

Sophie's eyes grew wide and she put her hands on her hips and stared at Ben. Aiyana took Sophie by the arm and led her away.

"Don't pay attention to him," she said. "He probably doesn't even know how to play four-square."

Suddenly, showing Ben around the school didn't feel like such a great job to Dakota. Still, it was his job. Just then the bell rang to let kids know that recess was over. Without much enthusiasm, Dakota motioned to Ben which way to go to line up.

After school, Dakota found his mother at the table

making dough balls. He knew what that meant.

"Cool! Fresh fry bread tonight!" he said with delight.

"Want to help?" his mother asked.

Dakota loved being in the kitchen with his mother. He thought she was the best cook in the world. Mostly, though, he just loved hanging out with her. He thought that she always smelled good and she was always warm. For Dakota, there was nothing better than a big hug from his mother on a cold day to warm him up fast.

His mother always told Dakota that he was her perfect son. She loved to remind him that he's fun, smart, brave, and loving. And he makes a mean fry bread, which in her book makes him a well-rounded person!

Dakota grabbed a handful of the sticky dough and began rolling it into a ball between his hands. He loved when his mother made the foods she grew up with. She always said that it reminded her of being a little girl and cooking with her mother and her grandmother.

She would describe the singing and drumming she would hear growing up, the smells of sweet grass and sage burning during prayers, the tiny house that her big family lived in.

"Mom," said Dakota, "when you were a little girl, did you ever have a new kid in school that you didn't like?"

His mother took the ball of dough from Dakota's hands, stretched it out into a saucer shape, and poured oil into a pan.

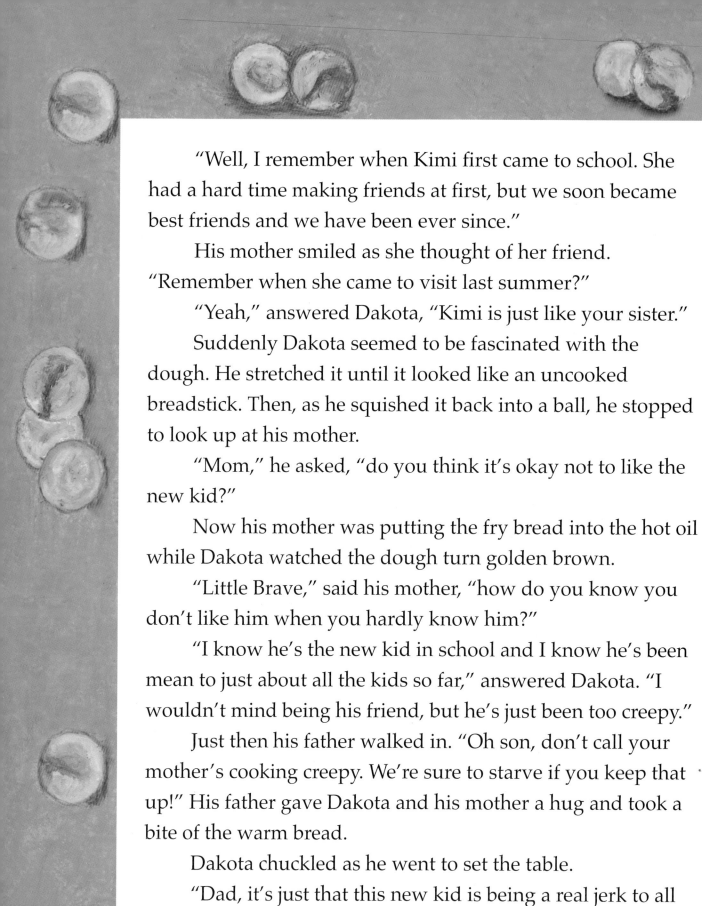

"Well, I remember when Kimi first came to school. She had a hard time making friends at first, but we soon became best friends and we have been ever since."

His mother smiled as she thought of her friend. "Remember when she came to visit last summer?"

"Yeah," answered Dakota, "Kimi is just like your sister."

Suddenly Dakota seemed to be fascinated with the dough. He stretched it until it looked like an uncooked breadstick. Then, as he squished it back into a ball, he stopped to look up at his mother.

"Mom," he asked, "do you think it's okay not to like the new kid?"

Now his mother was putting the fry bread into the hot oil while Dakota watched the dough turn golden brown.

"Little Brave," said his mother, "how do you know you don't like him when you hardly know him?"

"I know he's the new kid in school and I know he's been mean to just about all the kids so far," answered Dakota. "I wouldn't mind being his friend, but he's just been too creepy."

Just then his father walked in. "Oh son, don't call your mother's cooking creepy. We're sure to starve if you keep that up!" His father gave Dakota and his mother a hug and took a bite of the warm bread.

Dakota chuckled as he went to set the table.

"Dad, it's just that this new kid is being a real jerk to all the kids. I can't be his friend if he won't be mine."

Dakota's father tousled his hair and said, "Remember, son, if you want to get something, give it."

Dakota looked puzzled. He had heard his father say this many times, but he wasn't sure how it would help with Ben.

"Dakota," said his father, "you have always made friends easily. People like to be around you because you're caring and fair." His father sat on a stool next to Dakota. "I will always remember the day that the elders gave you your name at the naming ceremony. You surely cannot forget that your name, Dakota, means friend."

"I know, Dad," said Dakota. He loved hearing the story about when he was given his name back on the reservation, before his family moved to the city. "But how does that help me with Ben? He's not friendly or fair."

"Maybe you can teach him a thing or two about being a friend," his father said. "Our people believe in the circle of life. What you give away will come back to you."

That night, Dakota went to bed thinking about his father's words. The next morning he woke up with a plan.

At school, when Dakota saw Ben sitting alone at lunch, he told his friends that he was going to eat with him.

They all stared at him in disbelief. "Are you crazy?" they asked.

"Nah," answered Dakota. "I'm just going to give him

something."

When he set his tray across from Ben's he said, "I noticed you finished all the math today. You must be good at double-digit subtraction."

"Yeah," answered Ben, "math is pretty easy for me."

"So how do you like school? It's probably kind of hard being the new kid, huh?" asked Dakota.

Ben drank the last gulp of his milk and started packing up his tray.

"Especially when nobody likes me," he said.

Dakota looked surprised. "Well, we just figured you didn't like us — that's the way you were acting. So we left you alone."

Ben rolled his eyes. "That's just how I act. My mom calls me Mr. Tough Guy."

"Well, the kids don't really like Mr. Tough Guy. They'd probably like plain old Ben better," said Dakota. "If you want, I bet you could have lots of friends. You just have to give a little, that's all."

Ben squinted his eyes as he asked, "Give a little what?"

"Of whatever you want," said Dakota. "If you want friends, give your friendship to others. It's easy. Just say something nice, instead of mean, and watch what happens."

During recess Ben watched Sophie playing four-square with her friends. He looked at the ground and took a deep breath as he thought of what to say.

"Sophie," he started slowly, "you are really good at that. I noticed you hardly ever get out."

Sophie could hardly believe her ears. She just smiled and kept playing.

After school, Ben found Dakota and his friends in the middle of a marble game. He leaned on the wall near them and watched for a few minutes.

Antonio looked up and asked, "What are you looking at?"

"Um, you guys sure know some good tricks," he said. "Maybe you could show me one or two sometime."

Antonio looked at Dakota and shrugged, then looked back at Ben. "Well, do you want to play?" he asked.

"Sure, if it's okay," Ben answered.

He kneeled down and started picking out marbles. He and Dakota reached for the same green and gold striped marble. Ben got it first.

"Here ya go," he said as he handed it to Dakota.

"Are you sure?" Dakota asked.

"Yeah, you know how it works," answered Ben. He half-smiled as he looked at Dakota and added, "If you want to get something, you should give it. I'm sure I'll find another marble just as cool."

Dakota smiled at his new friend. "Yep, I bet you will."

Suki's Choice

Third Spiritual Law:

"When you make a choice, you change the future."

"We won! We won!" Suki yelled as she ran through the house. She was racing around the corner when she ran smack-dab into Father.

"Whoa! What's the big rush?" Father asked as he caught her with a hug.

"Are you running to get the last of the *mochi*? Because if you are, you're too late," he teased as he patted his stomach and smiled. "And it was delicious!"

Suki reached around her father to grab more of the *mochi* he was hiding behind his back. She bit into the gooey rice cake as she told Father about her day.

"I'm so excited! Today was our first class soccer game and my team won! Ms. Rey picked Eli and me to be team captains this week." Suki was talking so fast that she had to stop and catch her breath. "I got to pick our own team and everything!"

"Excellent!" exclaimed Father as he threw his hand in the air for a high-five.

"Now, Miss Team Captain, let's dig up something else to replace all that energy you used up in the game." He reached into a wooden bowl and pulled out an apple for each of them.

Suki hopped up to her favorite spot on the kitchen counter and told Father all about how she had made two goals and some great passes during the game. She was talking a mile a minute.

"My team was awesome! We'll be double ready for the school championships at the end of the month," Suki said as she crunched into the juicy green apple. "I knew just who to pick for my team. I made sure that Shy Shelly wasn't on my team. Good thing I got first pick."

Just then Father stopped her. "Wait a minute. Who's Shy Shelly and why didn't you want her on your team?"

"Shy Shelly is just about the quietest girl I ever saw. She never talks and she never plays with the other kids. That's why everyone calls her Shy Shelly. Plus she always gets picked last."

Father put down his apple. "Suki, I know you felt good when your team won. But what about her? How do you think Shelly felt being the last to be picked?"

Suki looked at Father and shrugged. "I don't know. I never really thought about it."

"What do you think would have happened if you had picked Shelly first for your team?" Father asked.

Suki thought for a moment. "The whole class probably would have been shocked."

"Mmm-hmm," nodded Father as he poured two glasses of milk. "And how do you think Shelly would have felt?"

"I don't know… pretty great, I guess," answered Suki.

Father put his arm around Suki's shoulder and gave her a hug. "*Suki-chan*, always remember respect and honor."

"Father, what does soccer have to do with respect and honor?"

"If you make choices that respect and honor yourself, your team, and Shelly, you will notice that everyone wins."

Suki thought about Father's words as she gently tapped her feet against the counter.

"Next time you're picking teams," Father added, "remember that when you make a choice, you change the future."

The next day at school Suki and Eli stood up to pick their teams for the day. Suki had been thinking about her talk with Father the day before. She thought about respect and honor. She thought about changing the future with her choices. As she stood up at the front of the class, she looked right at Shelly first. Shelly was looking down at her desk.

All of the other kids were bouncing out of their seats with their hands up yelling, "Pick me, pick me!"

Eli picked Kenji first and Kenji yelled, "Yesssss!" as he went to stand with Eli.

Suki had made up her mind. She took a deep breath and called out, "Shelly."

Suki heard her friends gasp. She looked out to see the whole

class staring at her. Then she looked at Shelly. Shelly looked surprised. At first she looked behind her to see if there was someone else Suki was looking at. Then she realized that the name called had been hers, Shelly. She looked wide-eyed at Suki as she pointed to herself and whispered, "Me?"

Suki smiled confidently as she waved her arm to motion for Shelly to come up and join her. Shelly couldn't hide her surprised smile as she made her way to the front of the class. She kept smiling the whole time Suki and Eli picked teams.

During the game, Shelly did something none of the kids expected. Every time the ball came her way, she walloped it down the field toward the goal! Their team lost by one point, but the whole class discovered Shelly's hidden talent. She was an awesome mid-fielder!

After the game, Shelly thanked Suki for picking her. "I had fun," she said. "Too bad we lost."

"Oh well," Suki said with a shrug and a smile. "I had fun too, Shelly. I had no idea you were such a good player! I'm just glad you were on my team! In my language we call that *subarashii*, spectacular. You were a spectacular soccer girl today," Suki added with a smile.

Suki held her hand up. Shelly hesitated for a moment before she responded with a high-five.

"Subarash--?" Shelly tried to repeat.

"Yep, *subarashii*," Suki confirmed.

Suddenly Suki's eyes lit up.

"*Subarashii* Shelly," she said with delight. "You have become Spectacular Shelly in my eyes."

Shelly giggled at the sound of it and repeated it slowly.

"Subara--shii Shelly," she said shyly. Her eyes looked up at Suki.

"It was fun to be on a team where I was wanted for a change," Shelly smiled.

Suki put her hand on Shelly's shoulder. "You can be on my team anytime," she said.

That night at dinner Suki told Father all about the game.

"Shelly even thanked me afterward," she explained with some surprise and pride in her voice.

Father was beaming. "So, how do you feel about your decision to pick her for your team?" he asked.

"It was kind of hard to pick her at first, when the whole class was expecting me not to. It felt like they were going to boo me out of the room or something." Suki laughed at the thought of that.

"But I'm sure glad I did," she added. "You should have seen the look on her face when I called her name. And who knew she'd be so good at booting that ball!"

"I bet Ms. Rey was proud of your choice," Father added.

"Yeah," Suki answered. "I gave her a suggestion. I thought that we would have fairer teams if we put everyone's name on a card and then picked cards for teams, instead of the old way of picking. That way nobody gets their feelings hurt and everyone gets respected and honored."

"It sounds like you made a great choice," Father said. "You made something better for Shelly and for yourself. And I bet you helped the other kids in your class learn something, too."

Suki dug into her rice and smiled. She knew she had done something great.

A Game for Hannah

Fourth Spiritual Law:

"Don't say no — go with the flow."

One Friday after school Hannah walked in, hung her backpack by the door, and headed for the stairs.

"Hi honey, no homework today?" her mother called after her.

"Well," Hannah paused midway up the stairs, "Mr. Solomon gave us a thinking assignment," she called back to her mother. "I'm going up to my room to think."

Mr. Solomon, Hannah's fifth grade teacher, was always giving the class thinking assignments. He reminded them often that they could come up with great learning experiences for themselves with a little guidance. Mr. Solomon loved to tell his students that they were their own best teachers. Hannah loved that about him.

At dinner when her mother asked her about the assignment, Hannah took a deep breath before she answered.

"Mr. Solomon asked us to think of something we could do for our community," she said. "He said it will be one of our projects while we're learning all about our city."

While she was talking, Hannah scooped up her long, wavy brown hair and tied it into a ponytail as she did each day. Ever since she found her hair dipped in the honey on her plate during last Rosh

26

Hashanah, the Jewish New Year, she had taken to tying it back before eating dinner.

Her little brother, Aaron, usually teased her about this. "Hannah, you spend like five hours before school getting your hair just right and after school you spend one second completely changing it," he would say in bewilderment. Then he usually ended with a sigh, "I don't get it."

"Don't try," Hannah rolled her eyes at her brother. She was convinced that her little brother would never get anything she did anyway. As far as she was concerned, she was light years ahead of him.

"The project sounds interesting, *maidela*," said Dad.

"Yeah," Hannah answered. She always felt warmer when her dad called her his *maidela*; she loved being his "little girl." "It reminds me about how *Bubby* and *Zayde* are always reminding us about *tzedakah* and *mitzvot*." Hannah's grandparents were always reminding her and Aaron about important values in their Jewish culture such as charity and doing good deeds, reminding them that doing even one *mitzvah*, a good deed, could make a big difference.

"Have anything in mind?"

"Not really," Hannah sighed. "A lot of the kids are going to pick up trash around the school or give their old clothes to some families who need them. Those sound good, but I really want to do something different."

"May I be excused?" she asked as she got up to take her

plate to the sink.

Then she waved her hand toward her family as she darted toward the stairs. "I'll just keep thinking," she said.

Hannah spent all of Saturday and Sunday trying to figure out what to do for her project. She walked through her neighborhood looking for an idea. She read the newspaper hoping for an idea. On Sunday, she even watched the television news searching for an idea.

On Monday morning, she dragged herself to the kitchen table to make an announcement.

"I'm not going to do it," she proclaimed in frustration. "I'll just take a bad grade."

"I bet Mr. Solomon would give you another day to think, if you asked him," her mother offered.

At school Hannah explained to her teacher that she hadn't thought of a project yet. Mr. Solomon agreed to give her a few more days. Hannah was sure she'd never think of anything. What was happening to her? She was starting to believe her brain just didn't work anymore!

That night at dinner, Hannah hardly touched her food. Dad had made his famous *matzo ball* soup, which she usually devoured. She loved to dip her *challah* bread into the warm broth. But not tonight.

When her parents asked her about the project, she told them she had some kind of brain block, and the whole thing was just giving her a headache.

"You know what's good for brain block, don't you, Hannah?" Dad asked with a grin.

"What?"

"Horseradish," he said as he pushed a small jar toward her. Dad had some kind of strange obsession with horseradish. "My secret weapon," he said as he reached into the cupboard and pulled out the matzo crackers and began to cover one with horseradish. "Brain food," he said.

Hannah rolled her eyes. "No thanks, Dad. I don't see how anyone could like that stuff," she answered.

"Oh come on, *maidela*. One bite of my secret weapon and you're bound to think of a project in seconds!"

"Yyyyyuck!" cried Hannah. "I'd rather have brain block than a burning mouth! I'll just stick to my soup."

"Okay, okay," said Dad. "But at least eat something. I suppose soup could be just as good for brain block. Besides, you need the energy to think."

"Face it," Hannah said as she took a small sip, "I'm never going to think of anything to do."

She was frustrated with not being able to come up with something. She took pride in being a straight-A student. Even though her parents always reminded her that she didn't always have to go for the A, she loved the feeling of having learned what she was supposed to as well as she could.

Her mother could see Hannah's frustration and wanted to help. "Hannah, why don't you turn it into a game?" she suggested. Her mother was good at making work feel like fun.

"Ugh," moaned Hannah. "How can it be a game when it's school?"

"Whenever you look around at people and places in our community, try to think of one helpful thing you could do to make a difference. You get one point for each idea you come up with. We'll all play and see who gets the most points," Mom added. "You're bound to come up with an idea you like for your project."

"Or at least a lot of points!" her brother Aaron chimed in.

Hannah slurped a spoonful of her soup as she considered the game. "Hmmm," was her only answer.

Her mother reached out to take Hannah's hand across the table. "Don't forget," she added, "when you feel good about doing something, it always turns out for the best."

The next morning on the way to school, Hannah noticed a man sitting beside a bridge with a backpack and a sign. She read it aloud: "Homeless, hungry, please help."

"Mom, how do people get to be homeless?" she asked.

Her mother thought for a moment as the traffic light turned red. "There are many ways that a person could end up with no home," she answered. "Someone might suddenly lose their job and have no money. And sometimes they have to ask others for help."

"Can't get much greener, Mommy," said Aaron as he watched the traffic light change.

"Wait!" yelled Hannah. "Don't go yet!" She opened up her lunch bag, took out her sandwich and chips, and got out of the car.

"Here ya go," she said to the man. "Hope you like turkey on whole wheat. Sorry, we were out of mustard this morning."

The man's eyes were grateful as he took the food. "Thank you, Miss. Turkey on whole wheat, hold the mustard, just happens to be my favorite." He gave Hannah a warm smile that made her feel great.

When Hannah got back in the car, Aaron said, "Way to go, sis. You just got a point! You just thought of one good thing to do for someone in our town."

"I just thought of my school project! I can't wait to tell Mr. Solomon!"

Hannah got an A+ on her project. She and her family spent Sunday morning making 300 sandwiches and the rest of the afternoon passing them out. The other kids liked the idea so much that each class in the school took one week to make sandwiches and deliver them to people around town who needed food.

When the local newspapers and television news stations found out about the school's efforts, they sent reporters to interview the students. Flash bulbs lit up the halls as reporters gathered details about the project. When one reporter asked Hannah how she felt about doing such a kind and helpful act for her community, she beamed.

"I feel great," she answered. Then she thought of her

mother and added, "Everyone knows that when you feel good about doing something, it always turns out for the best."

The reporter snapped Hannah's picture and said, "You know, young lady, that's a great way to get things done."

Tara Plants a Seed

Fifth Spiritual Law:
"Every time you wish or want, you plant a seed."

One Saturday while Tara and her family were hiking, she looked up and saw something strange on the mountainside. "Look at those tiny specks on the mountain. Are those rock climbers?" she asked.

"You got it," answered her dad. "Pretty brave, huh?"

Tara squinted as she tried to see the distant climbers more clearly. As she watched the specks moving slowly up the mountain, she made a decision.

"I'm brave. I'm ready!" she exclaimed. "That's exactly what I want to do! I want to climb a mountain!"

"You can do it," said her mom, "when you're a little older."

Tara and her little brother Raj had been coming to the mountains to hike with their parents ever since they could remember. Their parents liked to remind them that they had started hiking long before they could walk.

Tara liked hearing her father talk about how the mountains reminded him of where his family used to live in India. Both of her parents' families were from India. Although her parents were both born in the United States, they had gone to India to visit their families

and they told stories that their parents and grandparents told them of their native land, the mountains, the people, and their beliefs. They even taught Tara and Raj some common and important Hindi words now and then, but their favorite has always been *namaste,* the word you use when you say hello and goodbye.

Tara took pride hearing about this part of her family history and culture. She also shared her father's love of the mountains. She loved leading the hikes, pointing out wildflowers, and reading the trail signs about the area. Raj usually was content to lag behind a bit, just enjoying the scenery. He liked to say he was taking the scientific approach, studying the environment. Then again, he sometimes liked to pretend he was a superhero bounding up a mountain.

"It's a bird, it's a plane, it's Super-Raj!" he shouted.

"Raj, really, get a grip," Tara teased and then turned back to her mom.

"But Mom, I *am* older," Tara said as she ran ahead to regain the lead. She turned around to face her family, stretched her arms up, and stood as tall as she could.

"Look at me." Tara made her voice a little deeper and louder as she shouted. "I'm old!"

"Yes," smiled her mom as she put her arm on Tara's shoulder. "You are old, dear," her mom said. "But I mean when you're a few years older and a few inches taller."

"Why can't I do it now?" Tara turned to her dad, hoping he could see her readiness.

"Your mom's right," her dad said as he pushed aside a branch overhead so the family could walk through a narrow part of the trail. "You need to learn as much as you can about climbing first. You'll need special equipment and a lot of information and some practice," he said.

Tara jumped onto a big rock near the trail and cupped her hands around her mouth as she yelled, "LADIES AND GENTLEMEN, INTRODUCING THE WORLD'S GREATEST ROCK CLIMBER!" She threw her arms into the air above her head as she finished with a triumphant "TA-TA-DAH!" She looked down to see her family smiling and jumped down to rejoin her family.

The next day, Tara found her dad in the kitchen. "What's up, Dad?" she asked.

"I'm going to add some rosemary to our herb garden. Want to help me plant the seeds?"

"Sure," Tara shrugged. She picked out a small clay planter and poured in a little soil. Next she dropped a few of the tiny seeds into the pot and carefully covered them with more soil. Then she brushed her hands together to dust off the soil.

"All done," she said.

"Not quite," said her dad. "We still need to water them and give them a little plant food."

Tara watched him measure just the right amount of brown pebbles from the plant food jar and put the pot under the faucet.

"Why do we have to give them plant food right now?" she asked. "They're only seeds, not plants."

"If we want the seeds to be strong enough to sprout, we have to give them what they need to grow roots, like food, water, and light," said her dad. "These seeds are a lot like your hope to climb a mountain."

Tara squished her eyebrows together the way she did whenever she was confused. "What do you mean?" she asked.

"Whenever we make a wish or have a desire, we are planting a seed. We have to nurture our wish and make it strong. Just like the seed has to be strong to grow into a plant," her dad answered.

Tara chuckled. "You mean I have to water my wish to go rock climbing and give myself plant food?" she asked.

Her dad laughed too. "Sort of. If you really want to rock climb, you need to read about it, learn about it, and practice it. Then when you're ready, you'll be able to make your wish come true."

"Just like the seed will push through the soil and grow leaves when it's ready, huh?" asked Tara.

"You got it," answered her dad. "When your roots are strong enough, you'll be ready to climb a mountain."

That week, Tara went to the library and checked out some books about rock climbing. She read everything she could find, and when she finished she made an announcement. "I'm ready to climb a mountain!"

"I'd say your roots are pushing through the soil, but you're not growing leaves just yet," said her dad.

Tara sighed, "How long do I have to wait?"

"Well," said her dad, "do you have your gear ready? Do you have your ropes and climbing shoes and the other things you'll need on the side of the mountain? Have you practiced?"

Just then her mom got up from the couch and left the room. She returned with a pen and paper.

"I have an idea," she said. "Let's write down your wish to go rock climbing and all of the things you need to do to prepare yourself. Once a week, we'll check in with you to see what you've done to get ready. It might not be tomorrow, but you'll be able to see that you're making yourself as strong and ready as you can for when the big day comes."

"That's a great plan, we can all do it," said her dad. "We all have goals we want to accomplish."

During the next few weeks, Tara made plans for the big day, even if the big day was a long way off. She started saving her allowance for climbing shoes and gear. During dinners when her mom checked in to hear what everyone was doing to try to make their wish come true, Tara was ready.

"I've been saving my money for my gear," she said. "Oh yeah, Zoe said her dad is going to take us to the indoor rock-climbing gym with him sometime to learn all about it."

"Sounds like you have plenty of food, water, and sunshine for your seed," said her dad as he walked into the kitchen.

"Yeah," said Tara. "And you know what I figured out? That it's really exciting to make a wish and then help it come true."

Just then her dad peeked his head around the corner from the kitchen. "Tara, I just noticed that your rosemary plant sprouted its first leaves," he said.

"Yessss!" Tara yelled as she threw her arms in the air. "And pretty soon, so will I!"

The Lucky Tee

Sixth Spiritual Law:
"Enjoy the journey."

Dante's favorite Saturdays were the ones when he went golfing with Dad. Usually on weekends, Dante liked to hang out with Dad while his sister Malika went to do girl stuff with Mom. Dante didn't know what girl stuff was, and he mostly didn't want to know. Since their parents had divorced a couple of years ago, Dante and Malika got to have more special alone time with each of their parents.

Saturday golfing with Dad was pretty special to Dante. He loved spending the day outside, with Dad giving him tips on the game. Dad always told him that he had a beautiful swing, which made Dante beam with pride and want to keep playing even more.

Sometimes Dante focused too much on winning. It was then that Dad would smile and remind him that as long as he was having fun, it didn't matter what his score was.

Dante always brought along the special golf tee his favorite Auntie Adrienne had given him for his birthday. She loved to play golf too and liked to say that Dante had inherited his talent from her.

The tee was shiny gold with his initials engraved on it. Dante would hold the tee up to the sunlight to watch it sparkle.

"This is the shiniest gift I ever got!" he would say.

He used his special tee every time he played. He was convinced that it gave him good luck. Pretty soon he started calling it his lucky tee.

"I'll never play golf without my lucky tee!" he told Dad.

"Why not?" Dad asked.

"My lucky tee makes me play better!" Dante answered.

"Son, you were a good player before you had that tee, and you'd still play well without it," Dad said.

"Well, I'll never find out, because I'll always have it," Dante said with confidence as he put the tee into his back pocket.

At dinner that night, Dante told his mom and sister all about his golf day. "Daddy taught me a new way to hold my club," Dante explained as he buttered a piece of warm cornbread. "See?" He stood up to demonstrate the grip that Dad had shown him, pretending the butter knife was a golf club. "It really helped me swing better. Now I'll definitely win that junior golf tournament next week."

"Sugar, I'm pretty sure that the reason for the tournament is to let kids get together and have fun while they play golf," Mom said.

"And to raise money for the new community center," Malika chimed in.

"I know, I know, but with my lucky tee, I'm bound to win it!" Dante said as he reached into his pocket.

His eyes grew big as he checked all his other pockets. "My tee! It's gone! I put it in my pocket this morning! Oh no!" he yelled. He turned around and showed his family the problem. His finger was poking out of his back pocket.

Dante sat down and put his head in his hands. "I'll never be able to play great again!" he cried.

He jumped up and started looking around the house. "I have to find it! I can't play golf without it!"

Malika said, "Don't worry, Dante, we'll help you look."

The family searched all around the house, the driveway, and the yard. Finally, when it was close to bedtime, Mom called a halt to the search.

"Enough for tonight," she said. "The search can continue in the morning. How about some sweet potato pie before bed?"

"Mommy, I can't eat or sleep if I don't know where my lucky tee is," Dante said in frustration. "I have to call Daddy," he said as he reached for the phone and began to dial.

After hearing what had happened, Dad reassured Dante. "I can help you look again in the morning," he said, "but you can sleep tonight. And you can still play golf, even if we don't find it."

Dante hung his head and sighed into the phone. "I don't think so, Daddy," he said in a sullen voice.

"Dante," said Dad, "you're more than the things you have or don't have. You were a good golfer before you ever had that tee, and you'll be good without it."

Dante listened but didn't answer.

"You know, son, the things we have or don't have, like cars, toys, and lucky tees, don't really matter. The most important thing you have is you."

"I know that's important, Daddy. But I still think I need my lucky tee."

"And one last thing, remember you can be a good person with or without your lucky tee, or anything else."

Dante mumbled an unconvinced answer into the phone. "I don't know about that. 'Night, Daddy," he mumbled and hung up the phone.

For the next few days Dante moped around the house, occasionally looking under a table or lifting a chair cushion hoping to find his shiny good luck charm.

When he found Mom working on the computer, he even tried to lift the printer in hopes of finding it there.

"Dante," Mom said as she helped him gently set the printer back down, "unless your lucky golden tee grew tiny little golden legs, I don't think you're going to find it there."

Discouraged, Dante asked, "Mom, do you think I can still win that tournament on Saturday?"

Mom shooed his hand from the printer with a smile. "I think that as long as you concentrate on your game and have fun, you'll be a winner," said Mom. "Even if you don't take first place."

"Yeah, but I want to know how the tournament's going to go," said Dante.

"Then why play in the tournament at all?" asked Mom. "If you want to make sure you're always the winner, you should just play by yourself. That way you'll always know how the game will end up and who will win."

"Well that's no fun!" Dante answered.

"Exactly," Mom laughed as she took Dante's hand in hers. "It can be fun to be uncertain of the future. It keeps life interesting if we don't always know how things will turn out."

Dante thought for a moment. "So I should just try to do my best and not worry about how it will turn out, huh?"

"You got it," Mom answered.

Finally, the big day arrived. On Saturday Dante was at the golf course a half-hour early so he could practice before the tournament. He hit three practice drives perfectly. It felt great! He was already having fun, and the tournament hadn't even started.

"Dante, those are three of the best drives I've ever seen you hit!" Dad exclaimed.

"Yeah," Dante said. "And I don't even have my lucky tee!"

Just then Dad pulled something shiny out of his pocket and held it out in the palm of his hand. Dante's eyes grew wide and he gasped when he saw what it was.

"My lucky tee! Why didn't you tell me?"

"I found it yesterday under one of the seats in the car. I wanted you to see that how you do or how you feel doesn't depend on things you have or don't have," answered Dad.

Just then Dante heard the announcer call his name to start the tournament. He picked up his golf bag and began walking toward the first hole.

"Don't you want this?" asked Dad as he held the gold tee out for Dante.

Dante studied the sparkling tee in Dad's hand before he answered.

"Nah," he said, "you hold on to it for me. I'm going to do my best and have fun. I don't need a lucky tee for that!"

The Scavenger Hunt

Seventh Spiritual Law:

"You are here for a reason."

Zack and Savana could hardly wait!

"How much longer?" they asked from the back seat. They had been looking forward to this camping trip all week. This was their third year in a row to come to this lakeside campground with the other families.

As they turned into the campground, Savana asked Mom the same question she had asked her before they left. "Okay, Mom, spill it. What new and exciting thing do you have planned this time?"

Mom smiled and winked into the rearview mirror at the kids. "You'll just have to wait and see," she said smugly.

Savana turned around to look at the other cars following them into the campground. In the car behind her were her cousins Carlena, Tomas, and Trevor, with her Aunt Carmen driving. Behind her cousins was a car filled with their neighbors, Maya and Nicholas and their parents, whom Savana and Zack had known for as long as they could remember.

When the car stopped, everyone jumped out and started unpacking tents, cook stoves, sleeping bags, games, and food.

When the tents were set up and everyone had cooled off with

a quick dip in the lake, Savana asked, "Should we start the campfire?"

"Actually," Mom answered, "we all have something else to do before that."

"Aha!" Savana cried as she pointed her finger into the air. "At last we find out the big event!"

Mom gave each of the kids a piece of paper and a bag and announced that they were having a scavenger hunt.

"A what-enger hunt?" asked Zack.

"A scavenger hunt," Savana giggled. "That's when we all look for certain things on a list, and whoever gets all the things on the list wins."

"Oh yeah," said Maya, "we had something like that on the first day of school. Mr. Singh had us look for things around the classroom."

"Okay," said Mom, "everyone works in a team of two. Draw a number out of this hat to find out who your partner is."

Zack pulled out a number first. "Three!" he announced. "All other threes meet me over here."

Savana picked a number next. "Three?" she complained. "I have to be on the same team with my *brother*?"

"It's okay, sis. We'll whup 'em!" Zack replied.

When all the kids had teamed up around the campsite, Mom gave instructions. "Everything you need to find is right around here, so no need to go far. Stay with your team. We'll all meet back here at five."

Zack stood at attention. "Got it!" he exclaimed. "Let's all synchronize our watches! Mine says 4:27."

"Okay, Mr. Synchronize, let's go," said Savana as she led Zack by the arm.

Within a few minutes, Zack and Savana had most of the things on their list.

"We have one big pine cone, one piece of bark, and a strange looking rock," said Zack. "What else do we need?" He reached over to read the list Savana was holding.

Savana read the list aloud. "One twig longer than three inches, five pieces of litter, and... one special talent or quality?"

Zack furrowed his eyebrows in confusion. "Well, I can understand the litter part. Mom's always getting us to clean up the environment." Zack smiled at the memory of their vacation at the beach last year. Mom had said no castle building or wave jumping until they had cleaned up the bottles and cans in the sand.

"But I don't get the special talent part," he said as he studied the paper.

Savana bent to pick up an old bottle cap and dropped it into the bag. "Not sure," she answered. "Let's think about it as we go."

Soon their pockets were bulging with twigs, rocks, and pine cones, and their bag was full of trash left behind by other campers. Zack sat down on a big rock.

"We have everything except the special talent thing," he said. Looking carefully at his watch, he added, "We have only 12 minutes to get back."

"I've been thinking," said Savana. "You know how Mom is

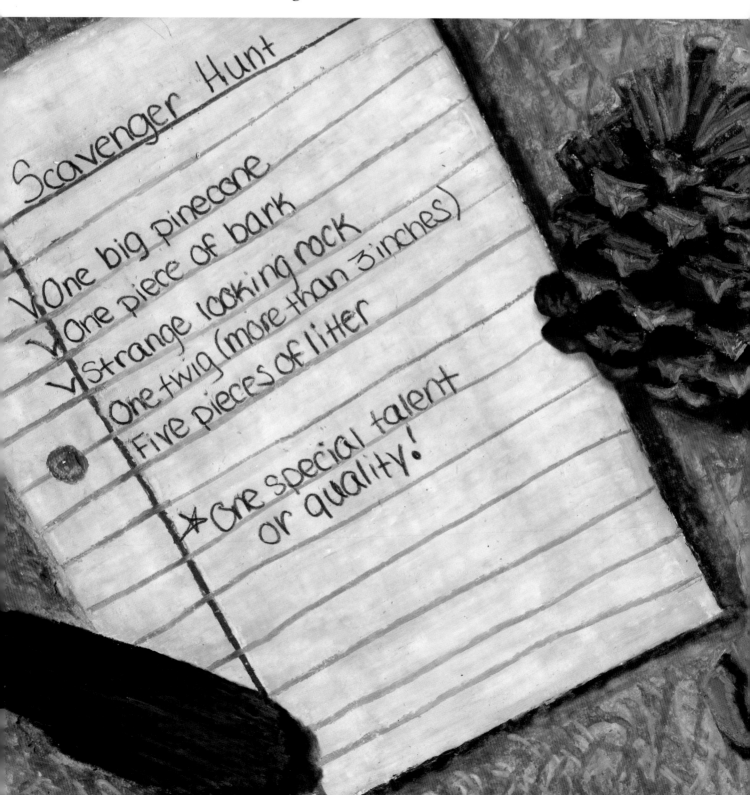

always saying we should notice the things that make us special? Like how we should be proud of being multicultural because we are part Latino, French, and Native American, and how that mixture makes us unique?"

"Y-y-yeah," Zack answered, still confused.

"Well, it's the same thing with finding a talent," said Savana with confidence. "I'm pretty good at dancing now. Remember how long it took me to get that first hip-hop routine at dance class?"

"Yeah, like pretty much your entire life," chuckled Zack.

"Whatever," Savana smiled back, "but I kept trying and practicing and finally got it right. Maybe that's what Mom means. She's always telling me I have determination, and that's a special quality and a talent."

With that, Savana got up, dusted off her pants, and took a step toward the campsite.

"Wait a minute!" Zack cried. "I haven't thought of a single thing yet! I don't do anything like that. The only special talent I have is blowing bigger bubbles than any of the other kids on the block!"

Savana held her hand out to help Zack down from the rock.

"I'm pretty sure you have more talents than bubble-blowing, little brother. In fact, you're good at a lot of things. Now let's head back while you think."

Back at the campsite, Mom was wrapping corn on the cob for barbecuing and Aunt Carmen was pouring her famous raspberry ice tea.

"Okay kids," Mom said, "set your findings on the blanket. We'll share our treasures during dinner."

Zack kept his head down as he kicked a small rock from one foot to the other. "I'm not ready," he said. "I'm still thinking about the special talent thing."

Mom put her arms around Zack. "You have so many," she smiled. "You're probably just trying to decide which to pick."

During dinner everyone shared about the things they had found.

"I really like the cool rock we found," said Zack as he held it up. "I think from all the colors that it might be jasper."

"Can we share our special talent now?" asked Savana.

"No!" cried Zack. "I'm still thinking!"

Savana looked around the group to see who would go first. Maya shared that she was really good at turning cartwheels until she was dizzy. Carlena told how she was proud of the way she played the piano her grandmother had given her, and the boys told about building, drawing, and racing. When it looked like everyone who wanted to had shared, Savana decided to speak up. She talked about how good she felt about her practically perfect dance routine and how she loved to dance until she dropped!

"It took a lot of determination for me to get it just right," Savana said. "I think determination is part of my special talent, too."

"That is a unique talent that you've put to good use," Mom said. "I've seen you teach your friends dance routines and help them until they get it right, too. That takes kindness and patience, two other great qualities you have," Mom added as she took Savana's hand and looked up to see a very frustrated Zack.

"I'm still not ready," Zack mumbled. "I don't want to give up, but I haven't thought of anything really good yet... except for my giant bubble-blowing."

Zack sighed, "I mean, I am good at a lot of stuff like baseball and skateboarding and making new friends and all that. But I can't think of a great talent or quality, like determination, kindness, or patience. Savana stole all the good ones! I have to work hard to get good at the stuff I do."

"Actually, I think you just hit on something," said Mom.

"What," Zack rolled his eyes, "figuring out who stole all the good ones?"

Mom smiled. "Well, that too. But one of your special talents is your perseverance."

"Per-se-what?" asked Zack.

"Perseverance. You keep trying things until you get them right even when you get discouraged. That's a very special talent," said Mom.

Zack's eyes lit up. "All right! I have perseverance!" he exclaimed.

He jumped up and cupped his hands around his mouth and shouted toward the trees, "I, Zack the Great, have perseverance! Perseverance!"

As he helped Savana collect the dirty dinner plates, Zack turned to ask, "Mom, why did you have us think about our special qualities?"

"Sometimes we forget how happy our special talents can make us and others," said Mom. "But we all have them and we should remember to use them."

"And now I'm going to use my special talent of being a *super-planner* to make everyone happy," Savana laughed as she grabbed her backpack and began taking out supplies.

"I brought everything we need for dessert... s'mores! Who wants to roast the marshmallows?"

"I will!" said Zack as he slid the soft white balls onto the roasting stick.

"Hey," he asked, "who won the scavenger hunt if we all found everything on the list?"

Savana looked up from the pieces of chocolate she was putting into the graham crackers.

"We all won, Zack," she said. "We each thought about our special talents and how we can use them to help others and to be happy. Anyone who can do that will always be a winner. Now, who's ready for dessert?"

Glossary

Abuelo—(ah-BWAY-loh) A Spanish word meaning grandfather (abuela means grandmother)

Arroz con Pollo—(ah-RROS con POY-yo) A dish made of rice with chicken

Bubby—(BUH-bee) A Yiddish word meaning grandmother

Challah—(HA-lah) Jewish egg bread

Chan—(CHAHN, as in Suki-chan) Suffix of endearment, usually for a girl's name

Hijo—(EE-hoe) A Spanish word meaning son (hija means daughter)

Hijito—(ee-HEE-toe) A Spanish word meaning little son, often used as a term of endearment

Hindi—(HIN-dee) A language spoken in northern India

Maidela—(MAY-duh-luh) A Yiddish word meaning young girl, often used as a term of endearment

Matzo Ball—(Mah-tzah ball) A round dumpling made from a coarse meal

Mitzvah—(MITZ-vuh) A Hebrew word meaning a good deed

Mitzvot—(MITZ-vote) A Hebrew word for more than one mitzvah

Mochi—(MOE-chee) A Japanese snack consisting of a sticky, round rice cake

Namaste—(NAW-maw-stay) A respectful greeting in India that means "the light and peace in me honors the light and peace in you"

Señor—(sen-YOR) A Spanish word for mister or sir

Subarashii—(sub-a-RAW-shee) A Japanese word meaning wonderful, splendid, magnificent

Tzedakah—(tzeh-DAW-kah) A Hebrew word meaning charity, such as giving aid, assistance, and money to the poor and needy

Zayde—(ZAY-dee) A Yiddish word meaning grandfather

Acknowledgments

Deepest thanks to my children, Savana and Zack, who inspired me to write this book simply by choosing me to be their mother. A huge, heartfelt thanks to Shendl Diamond, a phenomenal friend, artist, and visionary extraordinaire, who worked tirelessly and impeccably to bring this book to completion and who gently and not so gently reminded me to keep at it. Thank you, thank you for your love and generosity. Loving thanks to my dearest Sweet Billy for loving and supporting me through this project and for believing so strongly in my ability to succeed; to my mother, Catalina Caldwell, who has always encouraged me to go for it and who made me believe that I was the prettiest little girl in church all those years; to Hannah Shaffer for the remarkable talent that she infused into this book and for stepping up to a big challenge in such a remarkable way; to Deepak Chopra for his inspiration, teachings, and words of support; to Jennifer Chambers for her gracious support; to dear friends La Ronda Gumm and Ami Dougherty who have listened to all my rantings, supported my fantasies, and loved me through everything in between; to Bob Gadle, for the occasional big support shots in the arm; to Phil Lauder and Lisa Polikov for their fastidious and unrelenting editing; to Grant Powers for his belief and support in this project.

About the Author

Lora Ann, M.Ed., *Author*, considers being mother of her two children her most important and fascinating "project" to date. She also teaches literacy, life skills, yoga, and meditation to kids and adults. While working with Deepak Chopra at the Chopra Center for Well-Being, Lora developed a children's program based on Dr. Chopra's "Seven Spiritual Laws." Lora shares her passion for learning and teaching through workshops and seminars that empower others through her nonprofit organization, The Inner Wisdom Institute. As the published author of children's stories, short stories, educational articles, and a multicultural program for literacy and character development, Lora also mentors aspiring authors through LikeMinds Press (www.likemindspress.com). Her dreams include, but are not limited to, raising healthy, loving, and compassionate kids, world domination through peaceful and creative living, and unlimited toffee nut lattes.

About the Artist

Hannah Shaffer, *Illustrator*, is currently a high-school senior looking forward to attending university next year. Hannah is an extraordinary young woman who enjoys writing, painting, drawing, drama, and singing. Hannah is an honor student and was recently featured as one of *Delaware County's Young Emerging Artists*. She is also a member of the *National Honor Society* and the *National Music Honor Society*. Hannah is an avid reader and passionate about creating awareness and change in the areas of equality, environmental issues, human rights, and animal rights. She fesses up to an addiction to sugar cookies and Parmesan cheese, hopes to someday travel to Tibet to milk yaks, plans to own a pot-bellied pig at some point in the future, and believes laughter is life's medicine.